The Essential Travel Guide for Unforgettable Destinations

Timeless Sightseeing in Paris, The Captivating City of Light

Contents

Introduction 5

Practical Tips 6
Essential Preparations 7
Transportation and Getting Around 10
Cultural Etiquette & Local Customs 16

Landmarks & Monuments 19
Iconic Landmarks 20
Historical Monuments and Squares 25
Nighttime Charm & Illuminated Bridges 35

Neighborhoods & Districts 41
Le Marais – Historic Heart 43
Saint-Germain-des-Prés – Intellectual and Artistic Hub 48
Montmartre – Bohemian Paradise 53

Museums & Art 59
Louvre – Masterpieces Galore 61
Musée d'Orsay – Tribute to Impressionism 66
Pompidou Centre – Modern and Contemporary Art 71

Culinary Experiences 77
Boulangeries and Patisseries 79
Bistros and Brasseries 84
Food Markets and Gastronomy 90

Hidden Gems and Off-the-Beaten-Path 96
Secret Gardens and Parks 98
Artistic and Cultural Enclaves 103
Unconventional Museums & Collections 108

Day Trips from Paris   **113**
Château de Chantilly - Grandeur and Elegance   115
Versailles – A Royal Escape   119
Giverny – Monet's Inspiration   123

Common French Phrases to Know   **128**
Basic Greetings and Expressions   130
Ordering Food and Drinks   132
Asking for Directions and Getting Around   134

CONCLUSION   **136**

Introduction

Photo by Stephen Leonardi from Unsplash

Hey there, fellow travel enthusiast!

If you're anything like me, the allure of exploring new horizons and soaking in the rich tapestry of diverse cultures is an irresistible call. Join me on a journey through the pages of "The Essential Travel Guide for Unforgettable Destinations."

In this eBook, we'll embark on a virtual adventure to one of the most enchanting cities in the world – Paris, The Captivating City of Light. So, fasten your seatbelt, or rather, flip through the virtual pages, as we uncover the timeless beauty and unforgettable sightseeing opportunities that await in this iconic destination.

Get ready to be swept away by the magic of Paris!

CHAPTER 1
Practical Tips

Photo by Pedro Lastra from Unsplash

I now welcome you to the chapter we all secretly bookmark – "Practical Tips."

Think of this as your cheat sheet for navigating Paris like a seasoned traveler (even if you're a first-timer). From deciphering the metro map without breaking a sweat to finding that perfect café for your morning croissant fix, we've got your back.

No more wrestling with foreign guidebooks or getting lost in translation – just straightforward advice from one traveler to another. Let's dive in and uncover those nuggets of wisdom that'll make your Parisian adventure smooth sailing.

Essential Preparations

Photo by Dennis Rochel from Unsplash

Before you jet off to Paris, there are a few important things to get in order. Let's break it down step by step.

Visas and Travel Documents

First things first, make sure you have the right papers to enter France. Most North American, European (EU, EEA, UK), Australian, and New Zealand passport holders **do not** need a visa to enter France or the EU's Schengen free-travel zone of 29 countries for tourist visits of under 90 days, but it is essential you check your personal circumstances.

In addition:

- Ensure your passport is valid for at least six months from your planned return date, or you may be refused entry
- Make a digital or physical copy of your passport, visa, and any other important documents, such as a photo or photocopy.

This makes it much easier for authorities to provide assistance if you lose your travel documents

- Make a note of your country's Paris embassy details in case of an emergency.

Packing Essentials

Don't overstuff your suitcase – you'll want room for souvenirs. Remember chargers and travel adapters for your gadgets (France uses round two-pin type C and E plugs), and if you use any special medicine, bring enough for your entire trip.

- Check the current weather before you pack so you know exactly what to take
- Parisians dress elegantly even on a run to the supermarket. To blend in, pack 'smart casual' clothing – shirts are better than T-shirts for instance
- Layer up – the Parisian weather is changeable. Layering is the best way of being ready for baking sun followed by the wind that whips down the River Seine
- Bring an umbrella – it rains 110 days a year on average, right across the year
- Don't forget comfortable shoes for walking and exploring
- Pack a small first aid kit with band-aids, pain relievers, and any personal medications.

Travel Insurance

Travel insurance is a must in order to receive medical treatment in an emergency and cover the loss of items in the unlikely event they are stolen:

- Purchase comprehensive travel insurance with medical cover of at least US$1m, alongside trip cancellations, and lost belongings.
- Keep a copy of your insurance policy, policy number, and emergency contact information in your wallet or purse.

Money Matters

France uses the Euro (€), made up of 100 cents. €1 equals US$1.10. Euros can be easily obtained at home, and easily exchanged at banks and forex offices (bureau de change) for major currencies like the US dollar in Paris. Watch for forex stands near tourist attractions which offer a significantly worse rate of exchange to unwary travelers.

Electronic payments by debit/credit card are also increasingly common in the French capital. However, unless your card provider gives you fee-free purchases or withdrawals (there are ATMs everywhere recognizing international cards operated by Visa, Mastercard, and, to a lesser extent, American Express), you'll return home to an unexpectedly massive bill. You'll also need to notify your bank about your travel dates to avoid any issues with using your cards abroad.

Health and Safety Tips

Most travelers return from Paris with no issues, but it's worth noting the following:

- ✄ You need no special vaccinations to visit Paris
- ✄ Tap water is safe to drink, though you may prefer to stick to bottled mineral water
- ✄ Know emergency numbers – police 17, ambulance (SAMU) 15, fire 18. Or dial 112 for English-speaking operators. If roaming on your cell you will need to add the country code: +33 first
- ✄ Be aware of your surroundings, especially in unfamiliar areas, and avoid displaying valuable items
- ✄ For a city of 2.6 million people, Paris is incredibly safe, but pickpockets do target travelers, so use a money belt or hotel safe while being aware that police can ask for ID at any time.

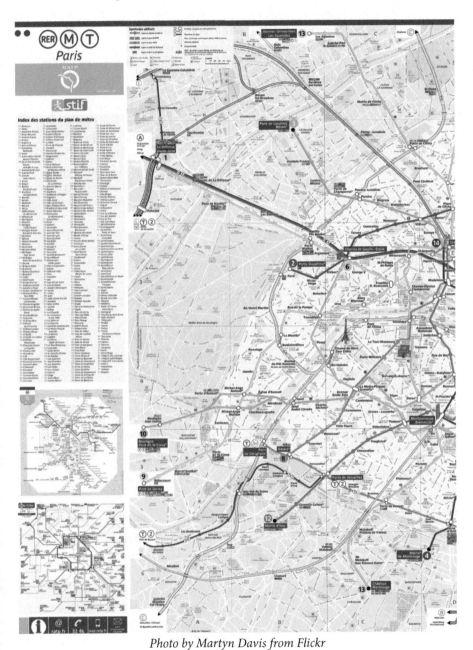

Photo by Martyn Davis from Flickr

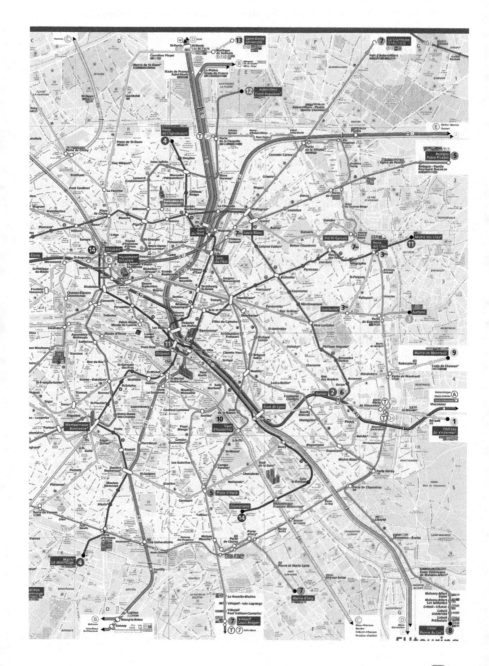

Whether arriving by plane or train, watch out for figures suggesting public transport or registered taxis are on strike. These people are almost certainly lying to get you in an expensive unlicensed cab.

Public Transport Overview

The Parisian public transport network is comprehensive, cheap to use, and not as scary as it looks. It comprises buses, the metro (subway), RER (a sort of metro to outlying suburbs), trams (streetcar/ trolley), rental bikes, and taxis.

- You'll rarely wait more than a few minutes for transport anywhere in the city

- Avoid traveling at rush hour (8–10am & 5–8pm) on lines heading into central Paris in the morning and out of Paris in the evening for the most comfortable journeys

- Operating times are roughly 6am to midnight daily.

Navigating the Metro System

By their nature, most metro stations are below ground, with limited accessibility for those with movement issues. They appear on city maps and signs as a yellow 'M'.

It can feel a little like a maze down there, given there are 16 lines and 300 stations. But don't worry – there are plenty of directional signs to help you figure it out.

- You need to buy a metro ticket before boarding and keep it handy throughout your journey. You'll need it to exit the station

- Every station has ticket machines with an English-language option

- A single journey ticket in central Paris costs just €2.10

- The Navigo Easy pass is a pre-paid card loaded with 10 journeys, taking some of the hassle out of repeated ticket machine visits

- The Paris Visite Pass offers unlimited use of public transport for 1, 2, 3 or 5 days
- The metro runs from 6 am till 12:45 am the next morning Sunday Thursday & 1:15 am Fridays and Saturdays
- Each line uses a different color, making this the easiest way of navigating the city. Trains show the last station in the direction of travel on their fronts.

Navigating the Bus System

Bus stops dot Paris, and the bus network is closely connected with the metro to the extent they use the same ticketing system.

- Buses generally run Monday to Saturday from 7 am to around 12:30 pm
- The Noctilien has night buses from half-midnight to around 5:30 am
- There is a reduced service on Sundays and public holidays, with some lines not operating at all
- Like on the metro, the line number and direction are indicated on the front
- You need to signal to the driver you want to board by extending your hand
- Tickets must be validated on the machines on board
- To get off, press the red button once
- Tickets can be bought at metro, RER, tram, and bus stations, but not at bus stops.

Using the RER and Tram Network

The RER (Regional Express Network) has five lines operating at the same times as the metro. From a tourist point of view, it's most likely to be used for getting between major stations (such as the Gare du Nord and Gare de l'Est) or for getting to the Palace of Versailles.

- The entrance to the palace is a ten minute walk from Versailles Château Rive Gauche on the C (yellow) line, with other stops including Champs de Mars, Invalides, Musée d'Orsay
- There are 13 tram lines (T1-T13), largely designed to serve the outskirts of the city.

Cycling in Paris

If you're feeling sporty, you can rent a bike. Biking in Paris is like a mini adventure. There are 3,700 miles of special lanes for bikes in and around Paris, meaning you can safely pedal around the city while feeling the breeze in your hair.

- City authorities run the Vélib' Metropole bike hire scheme with docking points all around Paris providing green (standard) and blue (electric) bikes from €3 for 45 minutes
- Other providers include Véligo, a docking station-free scheme using an app to locate the nearest free bikes.

Taxis and Ride-Sharing Services

Photo by Diego Fernandez from Unsplash

You're never far from a taxi rank in Paris, hosting registered metered taxis.

- They can also be hailed from the roadside, but not when close to a taxi rank or a bus stop
- Free (empty) taxis show a green light
- You'll need to pay in cash
- If you call a cab, the meter starts from that moment
- Alternatives include ride-hailing app Uber (but not Lyft)

Walking Tours and Routes

Walking is one of the best ways of discovering Paris. There are endless routes to choose from, official and unofficial. Following the Seine through central Paris is a favorite of ours.

- If you're in need of guidance, free walking tours (a donation will be expected) span a variety of areas including Montmartre, the Latin Quarter, Marais and all the main city center sights
- Wear comfortable shoes for walking and explore the city on foot.

Cultural Etiquette & Local Customs

Photo by Alicia Steels from Unsplash

When visiting Paris, it's not only important to explore the iconic landmarks and indulge in delicious cuisine but also to respect the local customs and cultural etiquette.

Understanding the way people interact, dine, and behave in various situations will enhance your experience and help you blend in with the Parisian way of life.

Greetings and Gestures

- **Bonjour:** The foundation of polite interaction in Paris is saying *"Bonjour"* (meaning "Good day") when entering a shop, a restaurant, or any public space. It's a simple yet crucial gesture that shows respect
- **La Bise:** When meeting friends or acquaintances, the common greeting is a light kiss on both cheeks, known as *"la bise."* The number of kisses can vary based on region and familiarity

✖ **Handshakes:** In formal settings, a firm handshake is appropriate for greetings. However, the two-cheek kiss is more common among friends and family

✖ **Eye Contact:** Maintaining respectful eye contact during conversations is considered a sign of interest and engagement.

Dining Etiquette

✖ **Table Manners:** When dining in Paris, keep your hands visible on the table, resting your wrists on the edge. Avoid placing your elbows on the table

✖ **Meal Times:** Lunch is typically around 12:30 to 2:30 pm, and dinner starts around 8:00 pm or later. Be mindful of these timings when planning your meals.

✖ **Ordering:** Politeness is key when ordering. Use phrases like *"S'il vous plaît"* (please) and *"Merci"* (thank you) to show appreciation

✖ **Bread Etiquette:** Place your bread on the table rather than on your plate. Tear off a piece and eat it, don't cut it with a knife

✖ **Wine:** When toasting, maintain eye contact and lift your glass slightly. It's also customary to say *"Santé!"* (good health!) before taking a sip.

Tipping Practices

✖ **Service Charge:** In most restaurants, the service charge is included in the bill. However, leaving a small additional tip is appreciated, usually rounding up to the nearest euro

✖ **Tipping at Cafés:** While not obligatory, leaving small change or rounding up the bill as a tip in cafés is a courteous gesture. You don't tip for drinks at a bar or club

✖ **Guides and Service Providers:** If you're happy with a guided tour or other services, a tip of around 5-10% is a kind of way to show appreciation.

Dress Code

- **Smart-Casual:** Parisians generally dress elegantly and neatly. When exploring the city, opt for smart-casual attire that is comfortable yet stylish
- **Respectful Attire:** When visiting religious sites or formal venues, it's advisable to dress modestly, covering shoulders and knees
- **Footwear:** Comfortable walking shoes are essential for exploring the city, but avoid overly casual footwear like flip-flops.

Respect for Historical Sites

- **Silence and Respect:** When visiting historical sites, such as churches or memorials, maintain a respectful demeanor. Keep noise levels down and turn off mobile phones
- **Photography:** While many sites allow photography, be sure to follow any rules or guidelines. Avoid using flash or tripods in museums and galleries
- **Cultural Sensitivity:** Some historical sites may hold religious or cultural significance. Be mindful of your behavior and attire to show respect for the local customs and traditions.

Now that you've got the basics down get ready for a journey through Paris's most iconic and breathtaking landmarks. From the towering Eiffel Tower to the intricate beauty of Notre Dame Cathedral, you'll uncover the stories behind these world-famous monuments.

Get ready to be swept away by the history, architecture, and charm of these awe-inspiring sites. So, keep turning those pages because the wonders of Paris are waiting for you to explore!

CHAPTER 2

Landmarks & Monuments

Photo by Soroush Karimi from Unsplash

Are you ready to embark on a journey through the heart of Paris, where every cobblestone seems to whisper stories of the past and every building stands as a testament to the city's enduring charm?

In this chapter, we'll guide you through the most iconic landmarks and monumental wonders that make Paris a true global gem.

But did you know? Paris is home to over 1,800 historical monuments, ranging from grand palaces to charming hidden gems. That's like stumbling upon a new treasure every day for nearly five years!

So, grab your map and imagination as we dive into the world of Parisian landmarks that have captured hearts and inspired dreams for generations.

Iconic Landmarks

As you step into the vibrant tapestry of Paris, you'll find yourself surrounded by an array of iconic landmarks that weave the city's history, culture, and allure together.

From the captivating heights of the Eiffel Tower to the artistic treasures within the Louvre Museum, each landmark offers a unique glimpse into the soul of this enchanting metropolis.

Eiffel Tower

An Icon in Iron

Photo by Anthony DELANOIX from Unsplash

The Eiffel Tower stands tall as the most recognizable symbol of Paris and a testament to architectural brilliance. Built by Gustave Eiffel for the 1889 World's Fair, this iron marvel reaches a staggering height of 324 meters (1,063 feet).

Ascend its elegant lattice structure via an elevator or a spirited climb, and you'll be rewarded with breathtaking panoramic views of the city's rooftops, the Seine River, and beyond.

As day transforms into night, witness the tower's spectacular illumination, a nightly homage to Paris's radiant spirit.

Louvre Museum

Artistry Unveiled

Photo by Mika Baumeister from Unsplash

Housing an astonishing collection spanning millennia, the Louvre Museum is a treasure trove for art enthusiasts and history buffs alike. This former royal palace turned museum boasts over 380,000 objects, including the enigmatic Mona Lisa and the majestic Venus de Milo – both of which are well signposted.

Stroll through the grand halls and corridors, marveling at works that span cultures, eras, and artistic movements. Remember, you might not be able to see it all in one visit, but every step taken within this cultural sanctuary is a step into the world's creative legacy.

Notre-Dame Cathedral

A Gothic Masterpiece

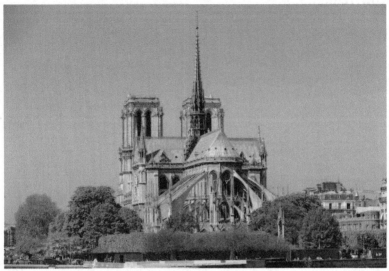

Photo by Sebastian from Unsplash

While recovering from the tragic fire of 2019, Notre Dame Cathedral remains an embodiment of Gothic splendor. Its intricate façade, adorned with stone gargoyles and delicate rose windows, is a testament to centuries of craftsmanship.

While temporarily closed for repairs, it's expected that by December 8, 2024, visitors will be able to step inside to witness the play of light through stained glass, feel the awe-inspiring height of the nave, and reflect on the solemnity of this historic sanctuary. In the meantime, its ancient shape can be admired from the little park of René Viviani across the river (and next to the famous bookstore Shakespeare and Company).

Arc de Triomphe

The Second-largest Triumphal Arch in the World

Photo by Rodrigo Kugnharski from Unsplash

Standing proudly at the western end of the Champs-Élysées, the Arc de Triomphe commemorates the victories of the French army and honors those who fought for the nation. Its sides are carved with dramatic French victories, while an eternal flame burns beneath the arch itself.

Climb to its summit to be rewarded with an awe-inspiring view of Paris's grand boulevards converging like spokes of a wheel. This grand arch, at the heart of the bustling city, serves as a reminder of France's resilience and unity.

Sacré-Cœur Basilica

A Sanctuary on the Hill

Photo by Saish Rane from Unsplash

Perched atop Montmartre Hill, the Sacré-Cœur (Sacred Heart) Basilica offers a serene escape from the city's hustle and bustle. Its stunning white domes and Romanesque-Byzantine architecture create an ethereal presence against the skyline.

Inside, the gilded mosaics and tranquil ambiance provide a moment of contemplation. And as you exit, enjoy the charming streets of Montmartre, an artistic district that has inspired countless creatives, from painters to street performers.

Historical Monuments and Squares

Each of these historic monuments and squares adds a layer of depth and character to Paris's narrative. As you explore their stories, you're immersing yourself in the tales that have shaped the city's identity.

Whether you're marveling at stained glass or delving into underground mysteries, let these landmarks guide you through Paris's rich tapestry of history and culture.

Sainte-Chapelle

A Stained Glass Marvel

Photo by Xuan Nguyen from Unsplash

Step into a world of ethereal beauty as you enter Sainte-Chapelle, another Parisian jewel of Gothic architecture. Nestled within the heart of the Palais de la Cité, this hidden treasure is renowned for its stunning stained glass windows that depict biblical stories in vibrant colors.

Bask in the kaleidoscope of light that dances across the interior, transporting you to a realm of awe-inspiring spirituality and artistic brilliance.

Panthéon

Hall of Greats

Photo by Kreshen on Unsplash

The Panthéon is a tribute to France's intellectual and artistic giants. Originally a church, it now houses the remains of luminaries like Voltaire, Rousseau, and Marie Curie. The impressive dome and neoclassical façade reflect the grandeur of its purpose.

As you walk through its halls, you're not only traversing architectural splendor but also paying homage to those who shaped France's cultural landscape.

Place des Vosges

Charm Amidst History

Photo by Pascal Bernardon from Unsplash

Nestled in the Marais district, the Place des Vosges is a charming oasis that blends history and contemporary allure. Lined with elegant townhouses, this square encapsulates classic Parisian elegance.

Find a seat on a bench or beneath a tree and immerse yourself in the tranquility of the surroundings, perhaps with a book or some people-watching – a timeless Parisian pastime.

Place de la Concorde

Where History Unfolds

Photo by Ozgur Kara from Unsplash

At the heart of Paris, the massive Place de la Concorde is a site of historical significance. The Obelisk of Luxor stands tall, flanked by majestic fountains and sculptures. This square has witnessed pivotal moments, from royal celebrations to the executions of King Louis XVI and Marie Antoinette during the French Revolution.

Walk its pathways, and let the weight of history mingle with the breeze as you admire the grandeur that surrounds you, from magnificent fountains to the fine neoclassical buildings that surround it.

Les Invalides

Monument to Valor

Photo by Pourya Gohari from Unsplash

Les Invalides is a tribute to France's military history and a resting place for its war heroes, including Napoleon Bonaparte. The golden dome of Les Invalides gleams under the sun, inviting you to explore its museums, galleries, and the tomb of Napoleon himself.

This complex not only showcases the nation's valor but also stands as a symbol of unity and remembrance.

Palais Garnier

Opulent Opera House

Photo by Caleb Maxwell from Unsplash

Prepare to be spellbound by the Palais Garnier, an opera house that exudes opulence and artistic grandeur. With its ornate interiors, intricate chandeliers, and lush red velvet, it's a masterpiece in itself.

Whether you're attending a performance or simply taking a guided tour, the Palais Garnier offers a glimpse into the world of refined elegance and artistic passion.

Place Vendôme

Elegance and Luxury

Photo by Romain Girot from Unsplash

A beacon of luxury and refinement, Place Vendôme is a square renowned for its haute couture boutiques and the iconic Ritz Paris hotel. The towering Column Vendôme at its center commemorates the triumphs of the French army.

As you stroll through this chic square, let the atmosphere of elegance and prestige envelop you.

Grand Palais

Architectural Marvel

Photo by Ştefan Jurcă

The Grand Palais is a symphony of glass and iron, a testament to architectural ingenuity. This exhibition hall and cultural center hosts a myriad of events, from art exhibitions and fashion shows for the greats of French couture to hosting fencing and taekwondo at the 2024 Olympics.

Its grandeur, coupled with its versatility, makes it a hub of creativity and a reflection of Paris's ever-evolving artistic spirit.

La Conciergerie

Whispers of History

Photo by Hugues Mitton

Experience the echoes of Paris's past within the walls of La Conciergerie, a former royal palace turned prison. Walk through its dimly lit halls, where Marie Antoinette and other prisoners were once held during the French Revolution.

This evocative site offers a glimpse into the city's tumultuous history and the lives of those who shaped its destiny.

Catacombs

Beneath the Surface

Photo by Travis Grossen from Unsplash

Delve into the eerie beauty of the Paris Catacombs, a maze of underground tunnels lined with the bones of millions. This macabre yet mesmerizing attraction showcases a unique perspective on history, art, and mortality.

As you navigate this subterranean realm, you'll uncover the enigmatic allure that lies beneath the city's bustling streets.

Nighttime Charm & Illuminated Bridges

As the sun sets, Paris undergoes a magical transformation, with its landmarks bathed in a soft, enchanting glow. In this chapter, we invite you to experience the captivating allure of Paris by night.

From leisurely cruises along the Seine to the romance of Montmartre and the dazzling lights of the Champs-Élysées, each experience promises to create lasting memories of the City of Light at its most beguiling.

Seine River Cruise

Glimmering Reflections

Photo from Hippopx

Embark on a Seine River cruise to witness Paris's iconic landmarks illuminated in all their glory. Glide under the illuminated bridges, passing the Eiffel Tower, Louvre, and Notre Dame Cathedral. The reflection of lights on the water adds a dreamlike quality to the city's most famous sights.

Whether you choose a dinner cruise, a sunset journey, or a simple evening ride, this voyage promises a unique perspective of Paris's beauty.

Montmartre at Night

Artistic Romance

Photo by Guillaume Didelet from Unsplash

Montmartre, the main artistic district, takes on a new level of charm after dark. The twinkling lights and narrow cobblestone streets create an intimate ambiance. The Sacré-Cœur Basilica atop the hill offers a breathtaking view of the city's sparkling skyline.

Explore the quaint alleys, listen to street musicians, attend a cabaret show at the Moulin Rouge, and let the artistic spirit of Montmartre ignite your imagination.

Champs-Élysées After Dark

Avenue of Radiance

Photo by Flynn Zhou from Unsplash

The grandeur of the Champs-Élysées is magnified as evening descends. As you stroll along this iconic avenue, the illuminated storefronts and theaters exude an air of elegance.

The Arc de Triomphe, standing proudly at one end, commands attention with its lights, while the bustling energy of the avenue offers a glimpse of Parisian nightlife.

Nighttime at the Eiffel Tower

Sparkling Heights

Photo by Stephen Leonardi from Unsplash

The Eiffel Tower, already a masterpiece by day, transforms into a shimmering jewel at night. Every evening, on the hour, the tower comes alive with a mesmerizing light show, where thousands of sparkling lights dance across its framework.

Find a spot at Trocadéro Gardens on the opposite side of the Seine to witness this magical spectacle and experience a moment of pure wonder.

Illuminated Bridges of Paris

Connecting Brilliance

Photo by Geoffroy Hauwen from Unsplash

Paris's bridges, each a work of art in itself, become even more captivating when illuminated. The Pont Alexandre III, adorned with golden statues and intricate details, is a sight to behold. The Pont Neuf, despite its name meaning "New Bridge," is the oldest in the city and comes alive with lights.

Walk along the banks of the Seine to see these bridges in their illuminated splendor, connecting the city's history with its vibrant present.

But hey! The journey doesn't end here. There's more to explore as we venture into the vibrant heartbeats of Paris's neighborhoods and districts.

From the cozy cafes of Le Marais to the artistic haven of Saint-Germain-des-Prés, you'll discover the pockets of charm that make Paris a tapestry of unique experiences.

So, turn the page, and let's delve into the neighborhoods that hold the essence of Parisian life, waiting to welcome you with their own stories and delights!

CHAPTER 3
Neighborhoods & Districts

Photo by Maksim Shutov from Unsplash

Just as Paris's landmarks light up the skyline, its neighborhoods and districts shine with their own distinct characters.

From the quaint streets of Montmartre to the trendy vibes of Le Marais, each corner reveals a unique facet of the city's personality. In this chapter, we invite you to wander through the charming neighborhoods that define Paris beyond its iconic landmarks.

In case you didn't know yet, Paris is divided into 20 administrative districts called *"arrondissements"* each offering its own flair and stories. Often likened to a snail shell when seen on a map, they spiral out in a clockwise direction from the 1er (first) arrondissement, centered around the Louvre, to the twentieth, in the Belleville neighborhood.

With more than 2,000 years of history, Paris's neighborhoods are like chapters in a fascinating book that tell tales of art, culture, and everyday life.

So, grab your walking shoes or bus pass, and let's explore the hidden treasures that make Paris a city of infinite discoveries.

Le Marais - Historic Heart

Nestled within the heart of Paris, Le Marais is a neighborhood that effortlessly bridges the gap between the city's storied past and its contemporary charm. Its cobbled streets, elegant squares, and vibrant atmosphere create a tapestry of history and modernity that captures the essence of Parisian life.

Place des Vosges

A Royal Haven

Photo by Pascal Bernardon from Unsplash

Step into the enchanting Place des Vosges, Paris's oldest square, and you'll find yourself surrounded by timeless beauty. With its harmonious architecture and tree-lined pathways, it's a peaceful oasis that once hosted French royalty.

As you take a leisurely stroll or rest on a bench, you'll understand why this square has been a favorite retreat for artists, thinkers, and dreamers throughout the centuries.

Le Marais Museums

Cultural Haven

Photo by Dario Gutiérrez from Unsplash

Le Marais is a haven for culture enthusiasts, boasting an array of museums that cater to various interests. The Musée Carnavalet offers a journey through Paris's history, while the Picasso Museum showcases the evolution of the legendary artist's work.

The Museum of Jewish Art and History offers insights into the neighborhood's Jewish heritage, making Le Marais a treasure trove of artistic and historical experiences.

Jewish Quarter

Rich Heritage

Photo by Guilhem Vellut

The Jewish Quarter of Le Marais is a testament to the diversity of Paris's cultural fabric. Explore the historic synagogues, wander through the charming streets, and savor authentic Jewish cuisine.

Delve into the stories of resilience, creativity, and community that have shaped this vibrant corner of the city.

Trendy Boutiques and Cafés

Stylish Exploration

Photo by ChrisGoldNY

Le Marais effortlessly balances its historic legacy with a modern flair. Explore its narrow alleys to discover trendy boutiques, artisan workshops, and stylish cafés.

From unique fashion finds to handcrafted souvenirs, you'll find treasures that reflect the neighborhood's artistic and fashionable spirit.

Local Stories and Legends

Whispers of the Past

Photo by Chahriar Hariri from Unsplash

As you wander through Le Marais's labyrinthine streets, you'll encounter intriguing stories and legends that have been woven into its fabric. From tales of hidden courtyards to whispers of famous residents, each corner holds a fragment of history waiting to be unraveled.

Engage with locals and hear their anecdotes, and you'll find that Le Marais's streets speak volumes about the soul of Paris.

Saint-Germain-des-Prés - Intellectual and Artistic Hub

Saint-Germain-des-Prés, with its timeless allure and bohemian spirit, has long been a haven for artists, thinkers, and those who cherish the finer things in life.

This neighborhood's elegant streets and rich artistic legacy make it a treasure trove of cultural experiences waiting to be explored.

Café Culture

A Cup of Conversation

Photo by Chahriar Hariri from Unsplash

Experience the heartbeat of Saint-Germain-des-Prés by embracing its legendary café culture. Sit at a street-side table, sip on a velvety café au lait, and watch the world go by.

Café de Flore and Les Deux Magots, once frequented by the likes of Jean-Paul Sartre and Simone de Beauvoir, not only offer beverages but a chance to absorb the intellectual and artistic atmosphere that still lingers.

Art Galleries

Gallery Hopping

Photo by Alice from Unsplash

Saint-Germain-des-Prés is a haven for art lovers, with numerous galleries showcasing a diverse range of works. From contemporary pieces to classical art, these galleries offer a glimpse into the creative pulse of the neighborhood. Among the best are the Galerie d'art Carré d'artistes Saint-Germain, LUMAS Galerie, and Galerie Vallois.

Explore the exhibitions, interact with artists, and maybe even buy artwork while discovering the boundless expressions that make Saint-Germain-des-Prés an artistic treasure trove.

Literary History

Words that Echo

Photo by Reza Rezvani from Unsplash

This neighborhood has a rich literary history that continues to resonate. Walk in the footsteps of literary giants like Albert Camus and Boris Vian, who found inspiration within these very streets.

The bookshops, such as Assouline and L'Ecume des Pages, pay homage to this legacy, making it a paradise for bookworms seeking to immerse themselves in words and stories as well as those looking for higher-end souvenirs.

Luxembourg Gardens

Tranquil Escape

Photo by Delaney Yan from Unsplash

Close to the bustle of Saint-Germain-des-Prés lies the serene Luxembourg Gardens, a lush oasis that offers respite from the city's pace.

Stroll along tree-lined paths, admire the exquisite statues, or find a spot by the fountains to read, relax, and watch the world drift by. It's a place where time slows down, and the beauty of nature takes center stage.

Iconic Streets and Addresses

A Walk Through History

Photo by Filip Mishevski from Unsplash

Every street in Saint-Germain-des-Prés seems to whisper tales of its past. Wander through Rue de Buci's market charm, Rue de l'Abbaye's historic elegance, and Rue Jacob's artistic vibe.

Discover the famed La Hune bookstore-turned-gallery and other iconic addresses that have left an indelible mark on the neighborhood's identity, from the Eugene Delacroix Museum and Church of Saint Germain to the Palais de Expositions des Beaux-Art museum.

Montmartre - Bohemian Paradise

Montmartre, with its whimsical streets and artistic soul, is a neighborhood that enchants its bohemian spirit. Perched on a hill, it's a place where painters, writers, and dreamers have found inspiration for centuries.

Come and join us! Lose yourself in the allure of Montmartre, where creativity knows no bounds.

Moulin Rouge

Vibrant Nights

Photo by Vadim Sadovski from Unsplash

Step into the colorful world of the Moulin Rouge, a legendary cabaret that has dazzled audiences since the Belle Époque. With its iconic red windmill, Moulin Rouge has been a symbol of entertainment and revelry.

Immerse yourself in a captivating show where music, dance, and extravagance create an unforgettable experience that echoes the exuberance of Montmartre's past.

Artist Squares

A Palette of Inspiration

Photo by Roman Kraft from Unsplash

Montmartre's quaint squares, like Place du Tertre, are artist havens where creativity spills onto the streets. Watch as painters capture the neighborhood's essence on canvas or perhaps commission a portrait as a cherished memento.

Engage with local artists, share stories, and witness firsthand the magic that transforms this corner of Paris into a living gallery.

Vineyard and Windmill

A Taste of Simplicity

Photo by GFreihalter

Nestled amidst the artistic bustle is the Clos Montmartre, a charming vineyard that offers a glimpse of rustic tranquility. The sight of grapevines and the Montmartre windmill evoke a simpler time.

Each year, the neighborhood celebrates the grape harvest with the Fête des Vendanges, a joyful event that showcases the harmonious blend of Montmartre's artistic and rural heritage.

Cabaret and Music

Melodies of Montmartre

Photo by Deigo Fernandez from Unsplash

Beyond the Moulin Rouge, Montmartre's streets come alive with cabarets and music venues that carry echoes of bygone eras.

Wander into cozy bars where soulful melodies fill the air or step into intimate theaters where the magic of live performances captures the bohemian spirit that has long defined this neighborhood.

Spirit of Amélie Poulain

A Touch of Movie Magic

Photo by Diego Fagundes from Unsplash

Montmartre's enchantment reaches beyond reality, thanks in part to the whimsical film "Amélie." The movie captured the neighborhood's quirkiness, cobblestone streets, and romanticism.

Walk in the footsteps of the film's protagonist and uncover the places that have become synonymous with the spirit of Amélie Poulain, adding a touch of cinematic magic to your Montmartre adventure.

As you've journeyed through the historic streets of Le Marais, the artistic haven of Saint-Germain-des-Prés, and the bohemian paradise of Montmartre, you've glimpsed the vibrant personalities that shape Paris's neighborhoods.

Each corner tells a unique story, from café conversations to artistic inspiration, inviting you to immerse yourself in the diverse tapestry of the city.

But our exploration doesn't stop here. In the next chapter, we'll delve into the world of Paris's renowned museums and art galleries, where masterpieces await your admiration. From the Louvre's majestic halls to contemporary galleries that pulse with innovation, you'll discover the art that has defined Paris as a global creative hub.

So, turn the page, and let's continue our journey through the captivating realm of Museums and Art in the City of Light.

CHAPTER 4

Museums & Art

Photo by Daniele D'Andreti from Unsplash

It's about time you step into a world where colors dance, sculptures speak, and history is etched in every stroke of a brush. In this chapter, we're diving headfirst into the vibrant universe of Paris's museums and art scene.

From the grand halls that house timeless treasures to the contemporary spaces that push boundaries, get ready to immerse yourself in a symphony of creativity that's as diverse as it is captivating.

Paris boasts more museums than you can shake an artist's palette at—over 130 in total!

If you were to walk the length of the artworks in the Louvre alone, you'd cover an incredible 9.7 miles. With this much artistic brilliance, you're in for a treat that will ignite your imagination and take your appreciation for art to new heights.

So, buckle up, art aficionados and curious wanderers alike, because the canvas of Paris is waiting for you to explore its myriad stories and expressions.

Louvre - Masterpieces Galore

Prepare to be swept away into the treasure trove of art and history that is the Louvre. With its iconic glass pyramid and expansive halls, this world-renowned museum beckons you to explore the vast panorama of human creativity spanning centuries.

Mona Lisa

The Enigmatic Smile

Photo by Mika Baumeister from Unsplash

When you come face to face with the Mona Lisa, you're not just admiring a painting; you're connecting with an enigma that has captivated minds for generations.

Housed within a climate-controlled enclosure, this masterpiece by Leonardo da Vinci radiates an aura of mystery that's as palpable as the iconic smile itself. Beat the crowds by visiting early or during the museum's less busy days.

Winged Victory of Samothrace

Graceful Triumph

Photo by Daniele D'Andreti from Unsplash

As you stand before the Winged Victory of Samothrace, you can almost feel the wind sweeping through her drapery. This Hellenistic sculpture of Nike, the goddess of victory, stands poised on the prow of a ship, embodying the exultation of triumph.

To truly appreciate the sculpture's grandeur, take a moment to observe it from different angles, allowing its dynamic energy to wash over you.

Venus de Milo

Timeless Beauty

Photo by Daniele D'Andreti from Unsplash

The Venus de Milo, with her missing arms yet enduring elegance, symbolizes the eternal allure of classical beauty. Carved in ancient Greece, she graces the Louvre with her presence, captivating visitors with her graceful form.

To appreciate the sculpture's details, move around it and observe how the play of light highlights its curves and contours.

Egyptian Antiquities

Journey to the Nile

Photo by R M from Unsplash

Explore the Louvre's Egyptian Antiquities on its lower floors to uncover the mysteries of ancient Egypt. From colossal statues to delicate artifacts, this collection offers a glimpse into the civilization that spanned millennia.

The renowned sphinxes, mummies, and hieroglyphics transport you to the banks of the Nile and the heart of a civilization steeped in symbolism and spirituality.

Artistic Interpretations

From Brush to Canvas

Photo by Heriberto Murrieta from Unsplash

Apart from housing ancient masterpieces, the Louvre also celebrates the creativity of countless artists with renowned artworks including David's *The Coronation of Napoleon*, Delacroix's *Liberty Leading the People*, and Vermeer's *The Lacemaker*.

These artistic dialogues across time invite you to contemplate the evolving nature of artistic expression.

Musée d'Orsay - Tribute to Impressionism

The Musée d'Orsay invites you to step into a world of color, light, and artistic revolution. Housed within a former railway station, this museum celebrates the transformative era of Impressionism and holds treasures that capture the essence of a dynamic period in art history.

Impressionist Paintings

Capturing Moments in Time

Photo by Diane Picchiottino

The Musée d'Orsay boasts an exceptional collection of Impressionist and Post-Impressionist paintings. Works by masters like Monet, Renoir, and Degas capture the play of light, the fleeting beauty of nature, and the candid moments of everyday life.

Take your time to observe the brushstrokes and let the vivid colors transport you to the heart of each scene.

Van Gogh Collection

Starry Night and Beyond

Photo by Redd F from Unsplash

The Musée d'Orsay showcases a remarkable collection of Vincent van Gogh's works, including a version of the iconic *Starry Night*. From his vibrant self-portraits to his emotionally charged landscapes, this collection offers a profound glimpse into the artist's tormented brilliance.

Don't miss the opportunity to witness Van Gogh's artistry up close.

Grand Clock and Architecture

A Glimpse of Elegance

Photo by Fernando Mola-Davis from Unsplash

The Musée d'Orsay's architecture is a masterpiece in itself, and the grand clock at its center is a symbol of the museum's unique identity.

As you stand beneath the intricate ironwork and look out onto the Seine, you're enveloped in the elegance of a bygone era.

Sculptures and Decorative Arts

Beauty in Every Form

Photo by Sara Darcaj from Unsplash

Beyond paintings, the museum's collection extends to sculptures and decorative arts. From Rodin's powerful sculptures to intricate Art Nouveau creations, you'll find beauty manifested in various forms.

Explore the galleries to witness the evolution of artistic expression and craftsmanship.

Stories of Artists' Lives

Artistry and Beyond

Photo by Manh LE from Unsplash

The Musée d'Orsay not only showcases artworks but also delves into the lives and stories of the artists behind them. Gain insights into the struggles, friendships, and inspirations that shaped their creations.

Audio guides and informative displays provide context that deepens your connection to the art and the artists.

Pompidou Centre - Modern and Contemporary Art

The Pompidou Centre is a renowned cultural institution celebrated for its focus on modern and contemporary art as exemplified by its 'inside-out' architecture.

Named after former French President Georges Pompidou, this avant-garde complex stands as a testament to innovation in both its architecture and the art it houses.

Striking Architecture

Architectural Marvel

Photo by Meizhi Lang from Unsplash

One of the most distinctive features of the Pompidou Centre is its unconventional architectural design.

Designed by architects Renzo Piano and Richard Rogers, the building's interior functions are turned outward, creating a unique exoskeleton-like structure. Its exposed pipes, elevators, and colorful façade challenge traditional architectural norms and make the building a piece of art in itself.

The National Museum of Modern Art

Art Through Time

Photo by Tom Podmore from Unsplash

Housing an extensive collection of modern and contemporary art, the Pompidou Centre's National Museum of Modern Art is a treasure trove of creative expression.

The museum showcases an array of works from the 20th and 21st centuries, featuring pieces by iconic artists such as Pablo Picasso, Salvador Dalí, Andy Warhol, and Jackson Pollock.

Dynamic Exhibition Spaces

Spaces of Innovation

Photo by Tetiana Shevereva from Unsplash

The Pompidou Centre boasts dynamic exhibition spaces that allow for the versatile presentation of art.

With its flexible layouts and expansive galleries, the center can host a variety of exhibitions, from large-scale installations to intimate displays, ensuring a constantly evolving and engaging visitor experience.

Street Art Influence

Urban Canvas

Photo by Emma Harrisova from Unsplash

Reflecting the urban and contemporary essence of its surroundings, the Pompidou Centre has been an advocate for street art and graffiti as legitimate forms of artistic expression.

It recognizes the significance of these art forms in reflecting the pulse of modern culture and often incorporates them into its exhibitions and programs.

Artistic Experiences and Workshops

Unleashing Creativity

Photo by zoetnet

The Pompidou Centre extends its engagement beyond static displays through a range of artistic experiences and workshops.

Visitors have the opportunity to participate in interactive sessions, workshops, and creative events that encourage them to explore their own creativity and gain a deeper understanding of the artistic process.

As we conclude this section on the captivating world of the Pompidou Centre, we've delved into the daring architecture that houses centuries of artistic innovation. From the striking façade to the dynamic exhibition spaces, this center embodies the spirit of modern and contemporary art.

But our journey doesn't end here. As we turn the page, we invite you to continue exploring the delights that await in Chapter 5: Culinary Experiences.

Just as art can stir the senses, so can the flavors and aromas of exceptional cuisine. Join us as we uncover the delectable treats and gastronomic wonders that Paris has to offer, blending artistry for both the eyes and the palate. Your adventure is far from over – let's indulge in the rich tapestry of tastes that await in the next chapter.

CHAPTER 5

Culinary Experiences

Photo by Fanny Prevost from Unsplash

Welcome to a chapter that promises to tantalize not just your imagination but also your taste buds! Just as a stroke of a paintbrush can evoke emotions, so can a perfectly cooked dish.

In this chapter, we'll journey through the delectable world of "Culinary Experiences," where art meets appetite in the heart of Paris.

Did you know that Paris boasts over 130 Michelin-starred restaurants? This city is truly a haven for food lovers, offering a spectrum of flavors that range from traditional French delicacies to innovative international fusions.

So, get ready to savor the stories, flavors, and aromas that make up the vibrant culinary tapestry of this enchanting city.

Boulangeries and Patisseries

It's time we embark on a delectable journey through the heart of Parisian culinary culture in this section, where we dive into the world of boulangeries (bakeries) and patisseries (pastry or cake shops).

You'll never be more than a few feet of them at any time – French law forbids it. But these charming establishments are more than just places to buy bread and sweets – they are repositories of tradition, craftsmanship, and creativity that define the art of French baking. Here's what to try:

Classic Baguettes

Photo by Michelle Ziling Ou from Unsplash

The iconic baguette, with its golden crust and soft interior, is the epitome of French baking. In boulangeries, you'll witness bakers perfecting the art of crafting these slender loaves that serve as the backbone of French cuisine.

A meticulous process involving the correct types of flour and to-the-minute baking times to achieve the perfect balance of airiness and chewiness, it's best to get there early in the morning to buy them still warm from the ovens.

Croissants and Pastries

Photo by Dana Marin (Amsterdamian) from Unsplash

Although not actually French but Austrian, there's arguably nothing more Parisian than the all-butter croissant (or 'crescent'). Indeed, a baker made international headlines recently for daring to make a vegan version.

Despite the name, it's the straight form of the pastry that is almost always made of butter, the curved version of margarine. Best consumed with a cup of black coffee, melt-in-the-mouth alternatives include pain au chocolat and fruit-filled Danishes (which also originally hail from Austria!).

Macarons and Sweet Delights

Photo by Melanie Kreutz from Unsplash

Vibrantly hued, exquisitely delicate, and ridiculously sweet, macarons are a symphony of flavor and texture. To our mind, there's no bad macaron, but for the very best in class, head either to a branch of Ladurée (there's one on the Champs-Élysées), L'Éclair de Génie (Boulevard Haussmann), or Maison Mulot (Rue de Seine), whose flavors include some of the most inventive out there.

Be warned, though, they don't come cheap, with each macaron costing anywhere from €1-2.50!

Beyond macarons, the patisseries of Paris are filled with sweet treats. Perhaps the best known is the chocolate éclair filled with fresh cream. Madeleine cakes are also well worth the calories, as are mille feuille – delicate layers of puff pastry interspersed with fresh fruit and cream.

Hidden Gems of Baking

Photo by Travis Grossen from Unsplash

It is so important they've got their own stores, not boulangeries or patisseries but creperies; the humble crepe also deserves our attention. Coming in both savory (seriously!) and sweet varieties, they can be bought takeaway from windows or enjoyed while sitting. For the very best, try Breizh Café in Le Marais, which has been serving up these pancakes for more than 25 years

Bistros and Brasseries

Step into the heart of Parisian dining culture as we explore the inviting world of bistros and brasseries.

These establishments offer more than just food – they provide a glimpse into the soul of the city, where classic French dishes, convivial ambiance, and heartfelt traditions converge.

Iconic French Dishes

Photo by Alex Harmuth from Unsplash

Bistros and brasseries serve as culinary time capsules, preserving and celebrating the rich tapestry of iconic French dishes. From coq au vin to boeuf bourguignon, French onion soup to veal steaks, these establishments bring comfort and nostalgia to every plate.

Many have inexpensive lunchtime menus, if not a huge amount of spoken English. You'll find bistros in every neighborhood (recognizable by their street tables and chalked-up menus). La Fontaine de Mars on Rue Saint-Dominique, Chez Georges on Rue du Mail, Le Bon Georges on Rue Saint-George, and chain Bouillon (there's one in Pigalle, a little south of Montmartre) all have exceptional reputations.

Wine Pairings

Photo by Jim Harris from Unsplash

The wine flows as freely as a conversation in Parisian bistros and brasseries. They may not have wine cellars to match more formal restaurants, but this being France you'll still have plenty of (mainly French reds) to choose between.

Bistros generally have a house wine (vin de la maison) on the go, served without pomp or the price tag of wines brought in.

Cozy Ambiance

Photo by Guillaume Didelet from Unsplash

Enter a world of warmth and familiarity as you step into a bistro or brasserie. These charming establishments are designed to embrace you like an old friend's embrace.

Wooden tables, dim lighting, and the hum of chatter create an ambiance that encourages relaxation and connection, making every visit a memorable experience.

Local Food Traditions

Photo by Anurag Arora from Unsplash

Bistros and brasseries often take inspiration from regional culinary traditions, celebrating local ingredients and recipes. From the hearty stews of the countryside to the seafood delights of coastal regions, these establishments pay homage to the diversity and depth of French cuisine.

Often family run, it's not unusual to find mama or papa in the kitchen out back, having visited the local markets for the freshest ingredients each morning.

The Soul of Bistros

Photo by Celine Ylmz from Unsplash

Beyond the food and decor, bistros and brasseries are vessels of stories, culture, and community. They are where artists find inspiration, friends gather for spirited conversations, and travelers experience an authentic slice of Parisian life.

In other words, you can't say you've visited Paris until you've spent a couple of hours people-watching from a bistro table.

Food Markets and Gastronomy

In this section, we'll take you on a culinary exploration through the vibrant world of food markets and gastronomy in Paris.

From bustling markets brimming with fresh produce to gourmet food shops that tantalize the taste buds, you'll uncover the heart of Parisian food culture.

Marché Bastille

Photo by Big Dodzy from Unsplash

Marché Bastille (Boulevard Richard Lenoir, a short hop east of Notre Dame Cathedral) is a quintessential Parisian experience that brings the city's gastronomic flair to life. Stroll through stalls overflowing with seasonal fruits, vegetables, cheeses, and meats.

The market's lively atmosphere captures the essence of local life while offering visitors a chance to indulge in the finest ingredients the region has to offer. One of Paris's largest and most traditional marketplaces, it's hundred or so stalls are busy with custom every Thursday and Sunday.

Gourmet Food Shops

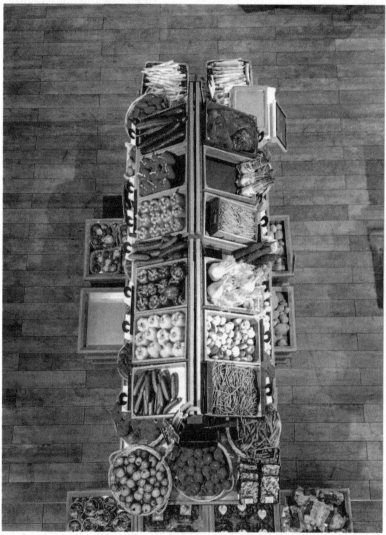

Photo by Serge Le Strat from Unsplash

Paris is a treasure trove of gourmet food shops that showcase the finest culinary offerings. Explore boutiques dedicated to exquisite chocolates, rare teas, artisanal oils, and other delicacies.

The easiest to visit as tourists are the food halls of the French capital's grand department stores, especially Printemps du Goût, La Grande Épicerie de Paris, and Lafayette Gourmet. Meanwhile, Maison Plisson (Boulevard Beaumarchais, near the Picasso Museum) has 6,000 different foodstuffs in stock, and **Causses (Rue Saint-Martin, Marais and Rue de Lorette, South Pigalle) combines a food store with a deli-inspired by the slow food movement serving up incredible sandwiches and other lunchtime delights.**

Fromageries and Charcuteries

Photo by Alex Guillauma from Unsplash

Delve into the world of fromageries (cheese shops) and charcuteries (cured meat and paté specialists), where the art of cheese and cured meats is meticulously honed. 'How can anyone govern a country with 246 varieties of cheese?' said wartime leader Charles de Gaulle.

Today, there are probably closer to 1,000 different types, from creamy Brie to tangy Roquefort, not to mention incredible numbers of perfectly aged hams and sausages. For cheeses, head to the likes of Fromagerie Laurent Dubois on Boulevard Saint-Germain, La Fromagerie on Rue Cler, and Fromagerie de Paris Lefebvre on Rue de Charenton, which are all very central. To-die-for charcuterie can be bought from chain Cul de Cochon including its Saint-Germain store, 100 year old Maison Vérot (multiple stores including inside Lafayette Gourmet), and Maison Thielen on Rue de Martyrs.

Culinary Fusion

Photo by Fanny Prevost from Unsplash

Parisian gastronomy has been shaped by centuries of cultural exchange, resulting in a unique culinary fusion. Experience the melding of flavors, techniques, and traditions from around the world as they blend harmoniously with French classics.

From Vietnamese banh mi to North African couscous, Paris embraces global influences while maintaining its culinary identity. The best place of the moment to try West African cuisine is Waly-Fay (Rue Godefroy Cavaignac), while the fantastic Kodawari Ramen (Yokocho) on Rue Mazarine is so cool it doesn't even take reservations (the fast turn around means you'll never wait long, but can't really linger either).

Rue de Bretagne's Chez Omar swaps the classic bistro menu for one of North African (nominally Algerian) delights, and Restaurant

Godjo (Rue de l'Ecole Polytechnique) serves up Ethiopian cuisine with distinction. In other words, whatever you hanker for, Paris can deliver!

Tales of Gastronomic Delights

Photo by Didier Provost from Unsplash

Food markets and gastronomy in Paris are more than just transactions; they're stories waiting to be savored. Engage with local vendors who are passionate about their craft, and you'll unearth tales of family traditions, culinary innovations, and the love that goes into each bite.

These stories enrich the experience and offer a deeper connection to the food you enjoy.

In Chapter 6, we will delve into a world of Hidden Gems and Off-the-Beaten-Path treasures that are waiting to be discovered.

Hold on tight because there's so much more to explore! In the upcoming pages, you'll uncover the stories behind these hidden wonders, learn how to uncover them yourself, and even hear from fellow adventurers who have stumbled upon these gems. Imagine the thrill of venturing beyond the ordinary, unraveling the mysteries that lie off the well-trodden tracks.

So, don't put the book down just yet. Turn the page, and let's continue this journey together.

CHAPTER 6

Hidden Gems and Off-the-Beaten-Path

Photo by Louis Paulin from Unsplash

Ah, Paris – the city of light, love, and legend. As you've strolled along the grand boulevards, marveled at iconic landmarks, and savored buttery croissants at charming cafes, you might have begun to think you know this city like the back of your hand. But wait intrepid explorer, there's more to unravel!

In this chapter, we invite you to swap the Eiffel Tower's queues for hidden courtyards where time stands still. It's time to venture off the well-trodden cobblestones and uncover the city's best-kept secrets.

Picture this: tucked away in the maze of Montmartre's cobblestone streets, you might stumble upon an artist's atelier echoing with stories of bohemian flair. Or, meander along the Seine's quieter paths to find bookstalls that hold the whispered words of generations past.

Whether you're a history buff, a culture vulture, or simply someone who craves that rush of discovery, this chapter will be your trusty companion. We'll help you navigate the labyrinthine alleyways, reveal the tucked-away bistros serving up culinary masterpieces, and lead you to vantage points that promise breathtaking views away from the selfie-stick crowds

Secret Gardens and Parks

Amidst the bustling streets and grand boulevards of Paris lies a quieter, more enchanting world – a realm of secret gardens and hidden parks. These verdant sanctuaries offer a tranquil escape from the urban pace, inviting you to lose yourself in the embrace of nature's beauty.

Let's embark on a journey through these hidden oases that whisper tales of serenity and seclusion.

Parc des Buttes-Chaumont

Photo by Yannis Sommera from Unsplash

Tucked away in the 19th arrondissement, Parc des Buttes-Chaumont is a well-kept secret cherished by locals. Designed by Alphand and Barillet-Deschamps, this park is a masterpiece of landscape architecture.

Picture lush hills, a picturesque lake with an island crowned by a temple, and romantic footbridges. As you wander through its winding paths, you'll discover hidden grottoes, waterfalls, and breathtaking panoramic views of the city.

Square des Peupliers

Photo by Chabe01

Escape to the 13th arrondissement and stumble upon Square des Peupliers, a delightful haven. This intimate park is a tribute to tranquility, named after the poplar trees that line its borders.

With its charming cobblestone paths, stone benches, and a serene pond, it's the perfect spot for a leisurely afternoon picnic or a quiet reading session.

Promenade Plantée

Photo by J Shim from Unsplash

Ever wondered about a park that floats above the city streets? Welcome to Promenade Plantée, a remarkable elevated garden located in the 12th arrondissement. Built upon a disused railway viaduct, this urban oasis offers a unique perspective on Paris.

Stroll through tree-lined pathways, admire vibrant flowers, and enjoy views of the bustling streets below – a truly novel experience.

Hôtel de Sens Garden

Photo by Nelson Minar

Nestled behind the historical Hôtel de Sens in the Marais district, this garden feels like a hidden treasure. The Hôtel de Sens Garden boasts an aura of old-world charm with its Renaissance architecture and lush surroundings.

As you step into this intimate space, you'll find yourself transported to another era, where the whispers of history and the fragrance of blooming flowers blend seamlessly.

Nature's Whisperers

Photo by User:Agateller

Venturing off the beaten path, you might come across the Nature's Whisperers project – a series of miniature gardens scattered around the city. These tiny marvels, often tucked into corners and crevices, celebrate the beauty of nature in unexpected places.

Created by anonymous gardeners, these pocket-sized green spaces offer a heartwarming reminder of the power of nature to thrive even in the most urban of environments

Artistic and Cultural Enclaves

Beyond the iconic Louvre and the vibrant Montmartre lies another layer of Paris – a realm where art and culture flourish in unexpected corners. These artistic and cultural enclaves invite you to step into the world of bohemian expression and creative innovation.

Join us as we unveil the hidden gems that pulse with the city's artistic heartbeat.

Ateliers and Studios

Photo by Sebastien Bonneval from Unsplash

Paris has long been a haven for artists seeking inspiration and community. Wander through the cobblestone streets of Montmartre and Le Marais, and you'll discover ateliers and studios that breathe life into the city's creative spirit.

Peek behind ancient wooden doors to find painters, sculptors, and artisans crafting masterpieces that carry the essence of Paris within their brushstrokes.

Street Art Tour

Photo by Rames Quinerie from Unsplash

While the Louvre houses timeless treasures, the streets of Paris themselves are a canvas for contemporary expression. Embark on a street art tour in neighborhoods like Belleville and the 13th arrondissement, where vibrant murals and thought-provoking graffiti tell stories of modern Parisian life.

These walls aren't just adorned with paint – they're adorned with the voices of today's artists.

Artist Communes

Photo by Clément Dellandrea from Unsplash

Hidden from the bustling boulevards are artist communes that offer a haven for creative souls. For instance, La Ruche is located in Montparnasse and has a history that echoes the footsteps of Chagall, Modigliani, and countless others.

Or almost countless – there are something like 15 artist communes spread around Paris, including Ateliers d'artistes de Belleville, Cité Internationale des Arts in Marais, and Maison d'art Bernard Anthonioz in Nogent-sur-Marne.

Most are only open on special days, but even so these communal spaces provide not just a place to work but also a nurturing environment where ideas are exchanged, collaborations bloom, and artistic evolutions thrive.

Cultural Hubs

Photo by Mbzt

Behind unassuming facades, Paris houses cultural hubs that celebrate everything from literature to photography. The Maison de la Photographie showcases captivating visual narratives, while Shakespeare and Company beckons bibliophiles with its cozy charm and rich history which makes it much more than just a bookshop (would-be writers can even stay the night thanks to the store's Tumbleweed program).

Inspirational Encounters

Photo by Valentin B. Kremer from Unsplash

Paris has an uncanny ability to bring creative minds together. Cafés like Café de Flore and Les Deux Magots have witnessed the conversations of literary giants like Hemingway and Sartre, while the historical Bateau-Lavoir was a melting pot of avant-garde thinkers.

Today, these spots continue to ignite sparks of inspiration, inviting you to sip coffee where art and intellect converge, and perhaps discover the greatest minds of the twenty-first century alongside your new favorite blends

Unconventional Museums & Collections

Prepare to delve into a Paris that defies expectations and celebrates the wonderfully bizarre. Beyond the Louvre's classical corridors, there's a world of unconventional museums and collections waiting to be explored.

From the peculiar to the extraordinary, join us on a journey through these offbeat realms that challenge your notions of what a museum can be.

Musée de la Chasse et de la Nature

Photo by Brett Hammond

Nestled in the Marais district, the Musée de la Chasse et de la Nature invites you to a one-of-a-kind experience that fuses art and the wild. This museum seamlessly blends taxidermy with contemporary art, where sculptures, paintings, and mounted animals share space in surprising harmony.

It's a place where the beauty of nature converges with human expression, leaving you with a sense of wonder that's both artistic and primal.

Muséc des Vampires

For those drawn to the mysterious and macabre, the Musée des Vampires offers a glimpse into the realm of the undead. This unique museum in Pigalle traces the history of vampire mythology through artifacts, literature, and pop culture.

From ancient folklore to modern movies, you'll explore the evolution of these enigmatic creatures and the enduring fascination they hold.

Musée de la Poupée

Photo by Pierre André Leclercq

Step into a world of dolls and dreams at the Musée de la Poupée in the heart of Le Marais. This museum boasts an enchanting collection of antique dolls, each with its own story and character.

From delicate porcelain creations to vintage Barbie dolls, the exhibits capture the artistry and cultural significance of these cherished playthings throughout history.

Curiosities and Oddities

Photo by Selbymay

Paris houses a treasure trove of curiosities and oddities that challenge conventional museum norms. Explore La Galerie des Moulages, where lifelike wax replicas of body parts offer insight into medical history.

Visit the Musée Dupuytren to see preserved anatomical anomalies and medical curiosities. These unconventional museums remind us that the strange and unique hold a special place in understanding the human experience.

Tales of Unusual Exhibits

Photo by ignis

In the City of Light, even the most ordinary objects can become extraordinary. Uncover stories of unusual exhibits like Le Musée des Égouts, where the underground world of Paris's sewers is illuminated.

Visit the Catacombs, where the bones of millions tell a haunting story of the city's past. These hidden attractions provide a visceral connection to the layers of history beneath the bustling streets.

As you close the pages of this chapter, take a moment to savor the secrets you've uncovered, the art you've embraced, and the unconventional wonders you've encountered in the heart of Paris.

You've ventured beyond the tourist maps, discovering hidden gardens that whispered tales of serenity, artistic enclaves that stirred your creativity, and museums that challenged your imagination.

But hold onto your curiosity, for there's more to explore in the pages ahead. Chapter 7 beckons, promising a new adventure just a train ride away.

We're about to unravel the treasures that lie beyond the city limits –
day trips that promise to transport you to medieval castles, charming
villages, and scenic landscapes that will leave you breathless.

Chapter 7

Day Trips from Paris

Photo by Kirsten Drew from Unsplash

Well, bonjour again, curious explorers! You've wandered the charming streets of Paris, savored the city's most delectable treats, and uncovered its hidden nooks. But guess what? The adventure doesn't stop at the city limits! Grab your beret, pack yourself a picnic, and hop aboard the train of excitement, because we're about to dive into the wonders that await you just a short ride away.

In this chapter, we're spilling the beans on the best day trips from Paris. Yes, you heard that right – there's a whole world of enchantment within a train's reach. Castles that seem straight out of fairy tales, villages that exude old-world charm, and landscapes that'll make your heart skip a beat – they're all here, waiting to sweep you off your feet.

You see, Paris isn't just a city; it's a gateway to a tapestry of experiences beyond its borders. Whether you're a history buff, a nature enthusiast, or simply someone who loves to escape the hustle and bustle, we've got a day trip that'll leave you with memories to treasure

Château de Chantilly - Grandeur and Elegance

Welcome to the land of fairy tales, where a magnificent castle and its sprawling grounds await your visit. Château de Chantilly is a place of grandeur and elegance, filled with history, art, and even a touch of equestrian charm. Let's step into this enchanting world and discover the treasures it holds.

Château and Grounds

Photo by Gilles Messian

Imagine a castle straight out of your dreams – that's Château de Chantilly. With its stunning architecture, beautiful gardens, and serene lake, it's like a picture from a storybook. The castle itself is like a time machine, taking you back to the past with its ornate rooms and intricate details.

And the gardens? They're like a paradise of greenery where you can stroll, relax, and soak in the beauty.

The Great Stables

Photo from Wallpaperflare.com

Hold your horses because the Great Stables of Chantilly are something special. These stables are not any old stables; they're like a palace of stables complete with a horse museum telling you all about these majestic animals.

And don't forget to meet the charming residents – the horses themselves, who are as friendly as they are elegant.

Art Collections

Photo by Dguendel

Art lovers, get ready to be amazed. Château de Chantilly is not just about beautiful buildings and gardens; it's also home to incredible art collections. Inside the castle, you'll find paintings, sculptures, and even rare books that tell stories from different times and places, including *The Three Graces* and *Madonna of Loreto* by Raphael, *The Ecstasy of Saint Benedict in the Desert* by Fra Angelico, and *The Guardhouse in Meknes* by Delacroix.

It's like taking a journey through the cultural history of Europe!

Horse Shows

Photo from Hippopx.com

Hold onto your hats – Chantilly is famous for its horse shows, most notably the Chantilly Classic taking place on the days immediately before Bastille Day on July 14. Showcasing the best horses and riders in the world on its tricky showjumping courses, there's still something to entertain the entire family, with an exhibitor village filled with stores, a food court, and a bar.

Equestrian Experiences

Calling all horse enthusiasts! At Château de Chantilly, you can dive deeper into the world of horses. You can watch dressage demonstrations, learn about horse training, and even try your hand at riding. Taking place in the Great Stables and lasting 30 minutes, these shows detail the secrets of equestrian expertise through commentary and riding to music.

Better yet, the demonstration is included in day tickets to the castl

Versailles - A Royal Escape

Step into the world of kings and queens, where opulence and history come to life. Versailles is a royal escape, just a short journey from Paris, and it's like traveling back in time to a world of grand palaces, magnificent gardens, and stories of royalty. Let's explore this regal wonderland together!

Palace of Versailles

Photo by Matthias Reding from Unsplash

Imagine a palace so grand it feels like a dream. That's the Palace of Versailles. With its glittering chandeliers, gold decorations, and grand halls, it's fit for royalty. Once the home of kings and queens, not least Louis XIV (the Sun King) and later Napoleon, it's like walking through history. Surrounded by elegance and luxury at every turn, it's still frequently used by the French President to impress important guests.

Gardens and Fountains

Photo by Armand Khoury from Unsplash

But the Palace is just the beginning. Outside, there are gardens that stretch as far as your eyes can see. These gardens are like a paradise of green, filled with flowers, trees, and even dazzling fountains that dance to the music. You can stroll, relax, and feel like you're in a fairytale.

Marie-Antoinette's Estate

Photo by Michal Osmenda

Did you know there's a special place within Versailles just for Marie-Antoinette? It's like her own private village! This part of the estate has little houses, a farm, and even a little lake. It's a peek into the queen's life and a chance to see where she escaped from the palace's grandness before her shocking end on the guillotine during the French Revolution.

Musical Fountains Show

Photo by Billy Wilson

Hold onto your hats! Daily between the end of March and beginning of November Versailles becomes even more magical with a musical fountains and musical gardens shows. During Musical Fountains shows the garden's elegant water jets dance to the music, and it's like a water ballet that will leave you amazed and delighted, while Musical Gardens shows tie walking tours of the gardens to music. They're a special treat that without doubt add a touch of additional enchantment to any visit.

Royalty and Intrigue

Photo by Jean-Philippe Delberghe from Unsplash

Versailles isn't just about pretty buildings – it's full of stories too. At times, the entire French court and administration lived and worked here; their lives were filled with drama, secrets, and even some mischief. Imagine walking the same halls where they made important decisions and had lavish parties. It's a chance to step into their world and discover the intrigue, so be sure to leave plenty of time to explore the palace's exquisite interiors too

Giverny - Monet's Inspiration

Get ready to dive into a world of color and nature where an artist's vision comes to life. Giverny, the place that inspired Claude Monet's paintings, is a short escape from Paris. It's like walking into a painting itself, where gardens bloom, water lilies dance, and the beauty of nature takes center stage.

Claude Monet's House and Gardens

Photo from Fondation Monet

Imagine visiting the house where a famous painter lived and worked. That's Claude Monet's house in Giverny. You can step into his world, see where he painted, and even stroll through the colorful gardens that acted as the base for the artist's famous water lilies series of paintings which can be enjoyed in the Musée d'Orsay.

Japanese Bridge and Water Lilies

Photo by Metzner

One of the most magical parts of Giverny is the Japanese Bridge. It's like a beautiful arch over a pond, covered in green plants and surrounded by water lilies. It's just like the paintings Monet made. Seeing it in real life feels like stepping into a masterpiece.

Impressionist Art Studio

Photo by Photolitherland

Monet wasn't just any painter; he was part of a special art movement called Impressionism. In Giverny, you can visit his art studio, where he created his amazing paintings. It's like a time capsule that takes you back to the days when art was changing and becoming more colorful.

Artist's Love for Nature

Photo by Pierre André Leclercq

Monet was in love with nature, and it shows in his paintings. He wanted to capture the colors, light, and beauty of the world around him. When you walk through Giverny's gardens, you'll understand why he was so inspired. It's like being in a living painting!

Capturing the Essence of Giverny

Giverny isn't just a place; it's a feeling. The gardens, the colors, and the peacefulness all come together to create a special atmosphere. You can't help but feel inspired by the beauty around you. Visiting Giverny is like capturing a piece of its magic and taking it with you.

Wow, what a journey it's been! From secret gardens to royal palaces, from hidden art enclaves to the inspiration behind famous paintings, you've explored Paris in ways you might not have imagined. The city has opened its heart to you, revealing its hidden treasures and stories that make it even more special.

But hold on tight because the adventure isn't over yet! In Chapter 8, we're diving into something super useful – common French phrases. You know, those magical words that help you connect with locals, order a croissant like a pro, and navigate the streets with confidence.

So don't put this guide down just yet. Turn the page, and let's dive into the world of language and culture. Chapter 8 is like your key to unlocking the heart of France even more. Ready to impress with your "Bonjour" and "Merci"? Let's continue this journey together and add a touch of French flair to your adventures

CHAPTER 8

Common French Phrases to Know

Photo by JOSHUA COLEMAN from Unsplash

As you've wandered through the enchanting streets of Paris, you've felt the city's pulse, tasted its delights, and explored its hidden corners.

But hold on tight because, in this chapter, we're diving into something that's like a magic key to unlock even more of the city's charm – the power of words!

In "Common French Phrases to Know," we're stepping into the world of language and culture. Whether you're a total beginner or you've dabbled in French before, this chapter is here to help you sprinkle a touch of French flair on your adventures.

The French have a reputation for rudeness – Parisian's especially –
but try your hand at French and they'll soon open up to you

Basic Greetings and Expressions

Photo by Yingchou Han from Unsplash

Let's start with the basics – the words that help you connect with people anywhere you go. Whether you're saying "hello" or "thank you," these simple words can make a big difference in your Parisian journey.

Hello and Goodbye

"Bonjour" (bohn-zhoor) means "hello" and "good day."

When it's time to say goodbye, you can use *"Au revoir"* (oh ruh-vwahr).

Please and Thank You

"Please" is *"S'il vous plaît"* (seel voo pleh) in French.

And when you want to show appreciation, say "Merci" (mehr-see) for "thank you."

Excuse Me and Sorry

When you need to get someone's attention or apologize, use *"Excusez-moi"* (ehk-skew-zay mwah) for "excuse me."

And if you make a mistake, "Désolé(e)" (day-zoh-lay) is "sorry."

Yes and No

"Yes" is "Oui" (wee), and "no" is "Non" (noh).

These are simple, but they help you communicate clearly. Plus, they're like little thumbs-up or thumbs-down signs in conversation!

I Do Not Understand

Not sure what's being said? Don't worry! Just say, "Je ne comprends pas" (zhuh nuh kohm-prahnd pah), which means "I do not understand." People will appreciate your honesty

Ordering Food and Drinks

Photo by Yousef Houssain from Unsplash

Time to satisfy your taste buds! Ordering food and drinks in Paris is a treat. Whether you're at a charming café or a fancy restaurant, these phrases will help you navigate the delicious world of French cuisine.

Restaurant Etiquette

When you enter a restaurant, always say "Bonjour" to the staff. To order, use "Je voudrais" (zhuh voo-dray), which means "I would like." And when you're done, "L'addition, s'il vous plaît" (lah-dee-syon seel voo pleh) gets you the bill.

Menu Vocabulary

Not sure what to order? "La carte" is the menu! If you see "Entrées," it's starters, and "Plats principaux" are main dishes. "Desserts" is for sweet treats!

Special Dietary Requests

Have dietary preferences? "Sans" (sahn) means "without." For example, "Sans viande" (sahn vee-ahnd) is "without meat." And if you're vegetarian, "Végétarien(ne)" (veh-zhay-tah-ree-ehn/enn) is your word, depending on whether you're a man or a woman!

Popular French Dishes

Want to try classic French dishes? "Croissant" (kruh-sahn) is a buttery pastry, and "Quiche" (keesh) is a savory pie. And if you're feeling fancy, order "Escargots" (es-kahr-goh), which are snails!

Toasts and Cheers

Ready to raise your glass? "Santé" (sahn-tay) means "cheers!" It's a wonderful way to share a happy moment with friends

Asking for Directions and Getting Around

Photo by Tomek Baginski from Unsplash

Time to explore! Whether you're wandering the streets or using public transport, these phrases will help you find your way and make the most of your Parisian adventure.

Asking for Help

Lost or unsure? "Excusez-moi, où est...?" (ehk-skew-zay mwah, oo eh) means "Excuse me, where is...?" Locals are usually happy to help!

Getting Metro Tickets

To travel on the metro, ask for "Un ticket de métro, s'il vous plaît" (uhn tee-kay duh may-tro seel voo pleh). And don't forget to say "Merci" when you get your ticket!

Finding Tourist Information

Looking for tourist info? "Où est l'office de tourisme?" (oo eh loh-fees duh toor-eezm) is "Where is the tourist office?" They can help you with maps and tips – and will speak English if you're struggling.

Exploring Neighborhoods

When you're ready to explore, "Je voudrais aller à..." (zhuh voo-dray ah-lay ah) means "I would like to go to..." Fill in the blank with the neighborhood you want to visit!

Navigating Public Transport

Using public transport? "Quel métro/bus pour...?" (kehl may-tro/boos poor) is "Which metro/bus to...?" It's a handy way to make sure you're on the right track.

So there you have it – a crash course in French phrases for your Parisian adventure! These words are like your travel companions, guiding you through greetings, dining, and getting around. As you use these phrases, you're not just speaking words – you're connecting with the heart of Paris and making your journey even more unforgettable.

Ready to add some French flair to your adventure? Let's dive into the world of language and culture together

CONCLUSION

Photo by Paul Matheson from Unsplash

As we come to the final page of this guide, it's time to reflect on the enchanting journey we've shared through the captivating streets, hidden corners, and grand wonders of Paris. From the Eiffel Tower's sparkling heights to the charming allure of Montmartre, from the serenity of secret gardens to the echoes of artists' dreams, and from the royal grandeur of Versailles to the blooming inspiration of Giverny – our adventure has been nothing short of magical.

Now, armed with the knowledge and appreciation you've gained, it's your turn to venture out into the world with the same enthusiasm and curiosity. Just as Paris has opened its arms to you, there are countless other destinations waiting to welcome you with their own tales and treasures. So let your wanderlust guide you, and may your travels be filled with the same sense of wonder that you've felt under the Parisian sky.

But remember that this is not the end – it's merely a pause in the journey. As you savor your memories of Paris, hold on to the lessons you've learned about embracing the unknown, seeking beauty in hidden gems, and opening your heart to the stories that cities whisper.

As we bid adieu to the City of Light, we leave you with a heartfelt farewell. The magic of Paris will linger in your heart – the whispered stories of cobblestone streets, the echoes of artists' laughter, and the warmth of the people you've met along the way. Carry these moments with you, for they are the lasting souvenirs that no suitcase can hold.

Thank you for sharing this journey with us. Your curiosity, your spirit of adventure, and your willingness to explore have made this experience truly special. Remember, wherever you go, let the lessons of Paris guide you – to seek beauty, embrace the unknown, and find the enchantment that lies within each step you take until we meet again.

Happy travels!

Made in the USA
Columbia, SC
25 March 2025